More praise for **Hey, Get a Job!**

"As an employability instructor to at-risk youth I find that Jennie Withers' book gives a terrific outline for our classes. Its interesting stories and youth-friendly language allow discussions and motivates questions. It is a necessity for our life skill classes."

Jaime Hansen ~ Student Advisor, Life's Kitchen

"This book is well written. The language, writing style and layout of the book will appeal to younger readers, but the information is relevant to job seekers of any age."

Jamie Simmons ~ Middle School Business Teacher, Christiansburg Middle School

"I would recommend this book to any educator interested in helping junior high or high school aged youth get and keep a first job. The book is laid out in a straightforward manner allowing a typical juvenile to easily create a résumé, cover letter, as well as be ready to fill out applications.

The book is an easy read that should grace your reference shelf."

Michael McKay ~ Idaho Department of Juvenile Corrections

Hey, Get a Job!

Author
Jennie Withers

Editor
Denise Dunlap-Taylor

Graphic Artist
Lisa Hlavinka

ISBN student edition 978-0-9842354-0-7
ISBN teacher edition 978-0-9842354-1-4

Hey, Get a Job!

HELP WANTED
(apply within)

jennie withers
author • teacher

The Rules of Life
By Charles J. Sykes
(A Perfect Place to Begin)

Rule 1:   Life is not fair, get used to it.

Rule 2:   The world won't care about your self-esteem. The world will expect you to accomplish something before you feel good about yourself.

Rule 3:   You will not make $40,000 a year right out of high school. You will not be vice-president with a hot car until you earn both.

Rule 4:   If you think your teacher is tough, wait until you get a boss.

Rule 5:   Flipping burgers is not beneath your dignity. Your grandparents had a different word for burger flipping; they called it opportunity.

Rule 6:   If you screw up, it is not your parents' fault, so don't whine about your mistakes. Learn from them.

Rule 7:   Before you were born, your parents were not as boring as they are now. They got that way paying your bills, cleaning your room, and listening to you tell them how idealistic you are. So before you save the rainforest from the bloodsucking parasites of your parents' generation, try delousing the closet in your own room.

Rule 8:   Your school may have done away with winners and losers, but life has not. In some schools they have abolished failing grades, they will give you as many times as you want to get the right answer. This, of course, bears not the slightest resemblance to anything in real life.

Rule 9:   Life is not divided into semesters. You do not get summers off and very few employers are interested in helping you find yourself. Do that on your own time.

Rule 10:   Television is not real life. In real life, people actually have to leave the coffee shop and go to jobs.

Rule 11:   Be nice to nerds. Chances are you'll end up working for one.

Rule 12:   Smoking does not make you look cool. It makes you look moronic. Next time you're out cruising, watch an 11 year old with a butt in his mouth. That's what you look like to anyone over 20. Ditto for "expressing yourself" with purple hair and/or pierced body parts.

Rule 13:   You are not immortal. (See rule No. 12.) If you are under the impression that living fast, dying young and leaving a beautiful corpse is romantic, you obviously haven't seen one of your peers at room temperature lately.

Rule 14:   Enjoy this while you can. Sure parents are a pain, school's a bother, and life is depressing. But someday you'll realize how wonderful it was to be a kid. Maybe you should start now.

You're welcome.

Introduction

Hello! So you've decided to see what it takes to get a job. I don't know how you got the book. Maybe you're an ambitious self starter who relishes the idea of being financially independent. Maybe someone gave you the book. If it was given to you, that's a pretty big hint don't you think? Either way, it's opened, so kudos to you.

> **Work saves us from three great evils: boredom, vice and need.**
>
> **~Voltaire, Candide, 1759**

I've tried to make this book as short and to the point as possible. I included cartoons, quotes and examples from teens. Everything I could think of to prepare you to enter the world of work.

I guess I should share my qualifications for writing this book. First of all, I've had a lot of jobs. My most recent occupation (besides a writer of this book) is a teacher. During the last five years of my fourteen year teaching career, I have taught a Technical Writing class for ninth graders. The class includes a unit on how to get and keep jobs. During my unit planning, I found tons of information for adults looking for careers, but very little for teenagers new to the work force. Because of this, I gathered bits and pieces of information from a lot of paper and internet sources, as well as talking to employers who hire teens.

*After I gathered all the material and put it together, I got the idea for **Hey, Get a Job!** I thought it would be nice to have age appropriate information on getting a job in one book and not scattered at job services, internet sites and in employers' heads. I also have to give credit where credit is due. Much of the book came from my students. I address five years worth of their questions, mistakes and positive experiences when getting and keeping a job. Thank you to my West students in Boise, Idaho.*

O.k., without further ado, here is what you can expect to see in your book.

Time to get off the couch!

Contents

Answers all those questions about what is legal for teens to do, finding openings and picking up applications.

The application you turn in is the employer's first impression of you. Don't make it their last. There's a lot of do's and don'ts I'll go over so your application doesn't end up in the trash.

There's a slim chance an employer may ask you for a résumé . Even if they don't, résumé writing is a skill you will need in the near future. I'll show you how to write one even with little or no work experience.

Part four will help you with the most nerve wracking part of getting a job, the interview. An interview doesn't have to be the stuff nightmares are made of. It's all about preparation.

So you get the job, then what? There are all these forms and things employers want you to learn before you start the job, one of those is the ability to read your paycheck.

Part six addresses what employers want from their employees. In other words, how can you avoid being fired?

There are things you should watch for to know whether you're being taken advantage of by an employer. This section also discusses how to avoid the pitfalls of having a job and making money.

STOP Throughout the book you will see stop signs followed by instructions to write. Use the Notes pages at the end of each section for these important assignments.

Frequently Asked Questions

I collected questions from my students as we talked about this information. I included the questions they asked, with the answers of course, at the end of each section.

So there it is. I would wish you luck finding a job, but it's not about being lucky, it's about being prepared. Congratulations on your intelligent decision to become a responsible, contributing citizen.

> *The will to win is important, but the will to prepare is vital.*
>
> *~Joe Paterno*

Section 1: *Who Will Hire Me?*

Teen who knows computers, team captain, Eagle Scout, taking business classes and Spanish,

WILL WORK FOR CHEAP!!

Hey, Get a Job!

Tasha turned sixteen and decided it was time to find a job. She immediately thought of the convenience store around the corner from her house. She knew the manager and thought it would be easy to get a job there because of this connection. Tasha asked her manager friend for an application. He told her he wouldn't hire her because the convenience store sold alcoholic beverages, and by law, Tasha was not old enough to sell them.

I'm sure I don't have to tell you, but teens aren't considered adults in the eyes of the law. So what does that mean when it comes to getting a job? It means you are restricted in what you can legally do for work, the age at which you can begin working, and how many hours you can work during school time and summer time. To find the rules for your state go to:

http://www.youthrules.dol.gov/states.htm
(click on the state in which you live)

Besides the laws given by the Department of Labor, individual businesses may set ages at which they will hire. It would be a good idea to ask if they hire teenagers, and at what age, before you fill out an application. If you are involved in an extracurricular activity like a sport, ask the employer if they will work around your schedule. There is no sense in filling out applications for jobs you have no chance of getting.

> *Do you know the difference between education and experience? Education is when you read the fine print; experience is what you get when you don't.*
>
> *~Pete Seeger*

Only 50 more years until retirement!!

Knowing what you can legally do helps narrow job choices, but you also need to think about what you want to do. Know yourself. Are you a people person? Are you good with kids? Do you like working with food? Do you want to be inside or outside? Are you restricted in times of day or year you can work? Think about your priorities. Don't lose sight of your long range goals like a state championship, high school diploma, or going to college.

It is true you can't be overly picky when it comes to your first job, but you also don't have to do something you will absolutely hate. It is a common misconception among teens that the only jobs available to them are in fast food restaurants or grocery stores. Those types of positions are often most visible, and they are great jobs, but they are not the only options. Don't apply for jobs you know will make you miserable. Why do that to yourself?

> *Knowing others is intelligence; knowing yourself is wisdom.*
>
> *~Lao Tzu*

Where To Look

Use the Job Service.

One resource not used enough by teens is the Job Service. As its title implies, its purpose is to help people find jobs. That includes teenagers. And, it's free. The Job Service can put you in contact with employers you may not think of. For students in extracurricular activities at school, those who want to focus on school work during the school year, and anyone who wants to work summers only, Job Services do summer job fairs for teens in the spring. They are also willing and able to assist you in locating a job year round. You can look up your state's Job Service on the computer or in a phone book. Keep in mind unemployed adults will take precedence over an unemployed teen.

> *Tom wanted a job, but didn't want to work in fast food or at a grocery store. Tom was an outdoors kind of guy. He also played school sports which would severely limit when he could work during the school year. Tom went to a job fair sponsored by his local Job Service in the spring. Tom found the perfect job working in the summer doing landscape maintenance for a school district.*

Use your connections.

Connections or word-of-mouth is also a good way to find a job. If someone knows you and your strengths, they are a good source for putting you in contact with employers. In a competitive job market where it's hard to get 'face time' with employers, a referral from someone you know can make all the difference. Be careful pursuing a job because a friend works there, however. I will discuss why a little later in the section.

Find it on the internet.

When I ask my classes where to look for job openings, many say the newspaper 'want ads'. Although this is a good source for adults, it tends not to be for teens. Businesses believe the newspaper is read primarily by adults; the want ads reflect that belief. The same goes for national job search web sites like Monster.com. If you can find a local area web site, you may have more luck there. There are web sites with job listings for teens out there. Do a search for 'teen jobs'. They cover mostly major cities, but they are worth checking into. The Job Service will post openings on the internet, but you need to register with them before you have access to those listings.

Research company websites.

Most businesses will list current job openings and instructions on how to apply either online or in person. Some will allow you to sign up for e-mail alerts for openings. Whether applying, submitting a résumé or requesting to be added to a mailing list, be sure to read all the instructions carefully so you don't make the wrong first impression.

Take a walk.

There is no law against simply applying at a business. If you think you would like to work at a certain place, ask them for an application. There doesn't have to be a 'help wanted' sign in the window for you to apply. Ask them to keep your application on file in case of future openings. Call periodically to make sure your application is still on file, and if an opening comes up, call and make sure they're looking at your application.

Be your own boss.

Have you ever considered starting your own business? One thing teens have going for them is they are cheap labor. Mowing lawns, babysitting, dog walking, cleaning, etc. are excellent ideas for teens. Make a pamphlet advertising your business and describing your qualifications. Distribute it around your neighborhood. See Section 3, *Don't Panic it's Just a Résumé* for ideas on what needs to go on your advertisement. You may be the perfect solution for your neighbors who are looking to save money on services. If you do decide to start something on your own, you are not going to escape the job process – you still have to sell yourself. Put an address, phone number, email and website address (if you have one) on your advertisement so that prospective clients may contact you. Because they are going to interview you before they hire you, make sure you are prepared. See Section 4, *I'm Speechless* for interviewing tips and be ready to discuss your qualifications and why they should hire you.

Consider volunteering.

In a down economy where jobs are scarce, and if you don't need the money, you may want to volunteer. Volunteering can be a great way to gain work experience. Some possibilities for volunteer work are at: hospitals, animal shelters, zoos, libraries, nursing homes, children's programs and any organization with non-profit status. You will have to apply and interview for volunteer positions because like employers, organizers don't want to waste time on someone who won't work out.

> *Paul was interested in the medical field, but wasn't sure specifically what he'd like to do. His parents made a comfortable living which freed him to consider volunteer work. He applied to volunteer at his local hospital. He was given a position where he helped discharged patients to their cars. He was good at what he did and it didn't go unnoticed. When a part-time paid position in the kitchen became available, Paul was asked to apply. He got the job. Paul helped prepare and deliver meals to patients. He loved his job and went on to become a nutritionist.*

Even if your volunteer position doesn't turn into one in which you are paid, there are other, perhaps more valuable payoffs. Volunteer work looks very good on applications for employment, college admissions and college scholarship applications. The money that you sacrifice now will be worth it in the future. You can't put a price on work experience, getting into the college you want or being awarded a scholarship. Besides that, volunteering makes you FEEL AWESOME!

 Make a list of what you want to do, places you will go to start looking for a job and people you know who might be helpful in your search.

Picking Up Applications

You should be at the point where you have a list of possible places to work. You will probably fill out several (minimum) applications before being asked to interview. The statistic I've read, keep in mind it's about adults and careers, was that less than 20% of applications received lead to job interviews.

Picking up applications is a lonely activity. Do not take anyone with you. If you want to scream immaturity, take a buddy or a parent with you to pick up applications.

> *I was leaving my local grocery store one day and passed the application computer kiosk on my way out. Sitting at the computer filling out a rather lengthy application was a young guy. Standing to the side of him, looking over his shoulder and helping him with his application, was his mom. Unbeknownst to either of them, the store manager was watching them work together on his application.*

My son needs a job.

It doesn't take a genius to figure out that young man will not get hired for the job. If he cannot pick up or fill out an application on his own, then what would make an employer think he could do a job independently? The point is you want to appear independent and mature. If you can't leave your mommy or your friends at home when trying to find a job, then you're not ready to be an employee.

Employers also don't like to hire friends. Every employer I've had, or those I've talked to, are afraid that friends will be more interested in being friends than they will be in working. Employers pay people to work, not to socialize.

Creating a Master Application

Before picking up applications, create a master application. Have all the information that an application may ask for. An easy way to do this is fill out the sample application in this book. In modern job hunts, many businesses have the application on a computer in the business. You will be expected to have the needed information readily available. It is a huge pain to memorize, or recreate each time, the information that goes on an application.

If it is an application you can take with you, pick up two. That way, if you mess up on one, you have a backup. Applications turned in with mistakes, cross-outs or white out on them are far less likely to get looked at.

Keys to Picking up Applications

- Know what you can legally do
- Have an idea of what you want to do
- Use resources available for teens to find job possibilities
- Go alone to pick up or fill out applications
- Create a master application

FAQs -Who Will Hire Me?

Does the economy affect teens' ability to get a job?

Absolutely! When the economy is in a slump, there is more competition for jobs because there are fewer of them. What this means for you is that you will not only be competing against others your age, but probably older people as well. Doing an application and interview to perfection becomes all the more important.

Can I go to a job fair with a friend?

Yes, but be serious. A job fair is not the place to start messing around with a buddy, or making out with your significant other.

Do temporary agencies work with teens?

Some do, some don't. It doesn't hurt to call. More of them will work with teens for summer employment. Be sure to also ask if there is a cost to you for their services.

How can I find what age requirements are at businesses?

Call them, or ask the next time you visit. They are happy to answer those kinds of questions for you.

If I have to be 16 in order to get a job I want, but I am 15 and my 16th birthday is soon, can I still apply for the job?

I would say that if your 16th birthday is within a week, go ahead and apply. You might want to tell the employer about your age situation when you turn in the application. Assure them you would be 16 by the time you started the job.

Will any of my jobs as a teenager help me with my future career?

Any job you have will help you develop social skills, work ethic and give you workplace experience. All those will help you in the future no matter what career you choose. As far as a specific career, you can look for positions that will do that. For example, if you want to be a dentist, then see if there are any openings in a dentist's office. You will impress the boss if you are interested in their careers.

Why can't teens under 18 drive for their job if they have a valid driver's license?

(This is an Idaho law, but is common in many states) Statistically speaking, teenagers are responsible for the most car accidents. This is probably due to inexperience as a driver. No employer wants to deal with that kind of liability.

Even though I can't drive for my work, can I drive to work everyday?

Absolutely. One of the questions that will be asked in the interview, or maybe even on the application, is how you are going to get to work. Employers want to know you have a reliable way to get there and back. Driving yourself is a reliable form of transportation, and the employer is not liable for what you do in your car if you're not on the clock.

Is there a rush to get a job right now?

In my opinion, no. Your parents may have a different perspective. Keep in mind there is a difference between not being ready and being lazy. One of the things I tell my students about their readiness has to do with references. If you cannot find three adults that can speak positively about your work ethic, you probably have some maturity issues that need some work before you're ready to get a job. That's just one of the measures, however. Some others are the way you feel about it, how you can juggle school and extracurricular activities and what your plans are with your family.

Notes

Notes

Education
Address
Name
activities
References
Training
Employment
Signed
Skills
Dated
Neat
there Can Be NO Mistakes

Hey, Get a Job!

> *If you want to achieve excellence, you can get there today. As of this second, quit doing less than excellent work.*
>
> *Thomas J. Watson*

The Application

The job application is an extremely important form. It is the first impression, and sadly, sometimes the only impression a person gets to make on an employer. Some applications are simple, and some are more complex. Some ask for references, some don't. Some even have quizzes attached. But whatever it entails, the application is not a place to be lazy. It may be your one and only chance. Like Life Rule #8 states: Your school may have done away with winners and losers, but life has not.

General things to know for every application:

- **If it's not typed into a computer, applications must be filled out in blue or black ink.** Do not vary from this even if pink is your signature color. If you fill out an application in anything but blue or black it will get thrown out.

- **Don't forget the date on the application.** All applications have a place for the date. If you don't know the date, ask.

- **Read the application carefully before you start writing.** Many applications have sections for the employer to write on. If you mistakenly write on these, employers are likely to toss your application because they don't want employees who can't follow directions.

- **Write neatly.** Employers are not like your teachers. They will not take time to decipher bad handwriting.

- **Don't abbreviate.** Many abbreviations are not common knowledge. It is a great idea to put things on your application like club memberships, but adults have been out of school for some time and clubs, as well as acronyms, have changed.

- **Don't leave blanks.** There should be no confusion of whether you missed a part of the application. To avoid this, use *N/A* which means not applicable, or *None*. Keep in mind there is a difference between *N/A* and *None*. *N/A* (not applicable) means it doesn't apply. If you put N/A next to college experience that literally means college doesn't apply to you. The employer is left to wonder why that is.

- **Check it over.** Remember, this is your first impression on the employer. Don't make it your last. Your application should have no misspelled words, be legible, have all blanks filled in, and there is no writing where it's inappropriate.

The Nitty Gritty Parts of the Application

These parts of the application are not in the same order on every application, nor will all applications ask for all of the information included here. Different formats mean you need to read the application thoroughly.

PERSONAL INFORMATION

Name:	Withers	Jennie	L.
	last	first	middle

Your name will be, besides the date, the first bit of information asked for. As far as your middle name goes, it's up to you whether to use it, use only an initial, or use nothing at all. It is also o.k. to put a shortened version or another first name you are normally called on the application.

Address:	1111 Curtis Street	Boise	ID	83702
	Street	City	State	Zip
Phone:	208-555-5555	Referred by:	Walk in	

Address is another necessary part of the application that should be a breeze. When it asks for street address, your house number goes first, 1212 Cherry Lane for example. When giving your phone number, make sure you put the number where you can be easily reached, or where you are sure to get a message. This is the number the employer will call to ask for an interview. If the number is your cell phone, make sure your ring tone and message are appropriate. Profanity, popular music and slang are not going to make you sound professional or even mature. Don't let the image you project via your cell phone hurt your chances of landing a job.

> *As a teenager you are at the last stage in your life when you will be happy to hear that the phone is for you.*
>
> ~Fran Lebowitz

Many applications would like to know how you found their job opening. Businesses often pay to advertise openings and they want to know if they are getting a return on their investment. If you saw a sign in the window, or just decided to apply, simply write 'walk in' in this space. As I mentioned earlier, referrals through contacts can be a great way to get a job, but you have to be careful about writing in a current employee's name for two reasons. One, if they are not a great employee, you are already judged as being not-so-good too. And two, employers don't like to hire friends. If you are applying because of a referral and you're not sure about the employee's performance, simply write 'walk in'.

EMPLOYMENT

| Position: Cashier | Date You Can Start: ASAP | Salary Desired: Open |

Applications usually have a section for you to tell the employer what you are applying for, when you can start and how much money you expect. As a first time worker, you need to answer these questions with care.

If you know the position, and you know they hire first time employees for that position, then write it in. If you don't know the specific position, simply write *open*.

The date you can start better be soon. You can write *ASAP* in this blank if that's the case. The openings you are going to be applying for usually need to be filled quickly, so you have to be prepared to start your new job within a month (maybe sooner) of applying.

As a first time worker with little work experience, you are not in a position to ask for a lot of money. It's a good idea to put *open* on this as well. Chances are you'll be offered minimum wage, but just in case the employer was going to offer you more, you don't want to let them know you would take less.

EDUCATION

Type of School	Name of School City, State	Date Attended	Graduate	Degree and Major Field(s) of Study
High School	Challis High School Challis, Idaho	8/06 - present	Yes ( ) No (x)	N/A
College	None		Yes ( ) No ( )	
Other	None			

For high school education, list the name of the high school you attend and the city and the state where it's located. For date attended, put the month and year you started high school to present. If you've moved or changed high schools, put the date you started high school as a Freshman. Mark *No* if it asks about graduation. Degree and major fields of study are going to be *N/A* because choosing a major does not apply to high school.

College and **Other** are both going to be *None*. You only need to write *None* in the first blank and that will take care of the entire row. Even if you take Advanced Placement courses in high school and will receive college credit, it is not the same as attending college. There will usually be a more appropriate place to list your AP stuff. **Other** is also post high school. Again, even if you take classes in high school that you can receive Vocational Technical credits for, it will go elsewhere on the application.

Don't be surprised if the application has a place for you to put your Grade Point Average, and/or the number of absences or tardies you have in school. Be honest, and be prepared to explain if either one of these doesn't look good. If you are tempted to fib, read the part of this chapter titled, 'Don't Be a Liar, Liar, Pants on Fire!'

SPECIAL SKILLS, TRAINING, OR ACTIVITIES

> Varsity Basketball, Honor roll – 2 semesters, Completed Computer Applications I and II, Spanish I, Volunteer for the Senior Center two hours per week, Welding I, Vocational Technical Professionals of America member

Whatever they call this section of an application, or however it is worded, it is the one place where you are able to set yourself apart from other applicants. Remember, you have only this piece of paper to make an impression. This is where you want to put extracurricular activities, honor roll, club memberships, extra courses you take in high school (like the Vocational Technical classes or Advanced Placement courses), volunteer work, awards you've received and even electives like computers or foreign languages you take in school. Do not leave it blank. Use it to set yourself above the other applicants.

EMPLOYMENT HISTORY

Date	Name, address and phone number of employer	Position	Salary	Reason for Leaving
From: To:	None			

At your age, no employer expects you to have an extensive work history. You can write *None* in one of the large boxes and take care of the whole section. However, you may count babysitting, lawn mowing etc. as work history if: 1) you worked for someone outside your family for an extended period of time, and 2) you received money for your efforts. Doing chores for an allowance doesn't count. Chores are a sneaky way your family uses to teach you about work ethic. Keep in mind, however, if you use people as former employers, you can't use them as personal references. At this point, it is more important for you to have personal references than it is to have a work history.

> *Teenagers who are never required to vacuum are living in one.*
> ~Fred G. Gosman

Date	Name, address and phone number of employer	Position	Salary	Reason for Leaving
From: To:	Daniel Smith 7878 Oak Dr. Boise, Id 82705 (208) 775-7612	Lawn Maintenance	$20/week	Current

If you do have employment history, you will need the month and year of when you started the job and the month and year when it ended. If it hasn't ended, you write *present* or *current*.

The name, address and phone number of the employer is needed. The phone number is particularly important so a prospective employer can make contact to ask about what kind of worker you are.

Position, salary and reason for leaving will also be asked. Position is simply what you did for the employer. The salary doesn't have to be per hour, but may be $20/job or $100/week, etc. For reason for leaving, it will be *present* or *current* if you are still doing it. It can also be *job ended* if it was only a temporary gig. If the answer is fired, then don't use it as work history.

REFERENCES

Name and occupation	Address	Phone Number	Years Known
George Jones Accountant	111 Apple Street Boise, Id 83655	(208) 444 - 3333	5
Ellen Smith Teacher	6567 Castle Drive Meridian, Id 83642	(208) 222 - 1111	1
Dow Dean Coach	12345 Baller Way Challis, Id 83445	(208) 777 - 8888	2

You will need to have three references. Some applications may ask for none, some one or two, and others three. In order to be prepared, you should have three that meet the following criteria:

• Must be adults! Believe it or not, employers don't care what your friends think about you because they are not adults who have been in the world of work.

• Don't use your parents or relatives. These people have a vested interest in whether or not you get a job. They want your butt off the couch helping to pay for your stuff, so of course they're going to say anything it takes to make that happen.

• Can speak about your work ethic. Even though your relatives won't work as references, there should be plenty of adults who can talk about what a hard working, great person you are. Coaches, teachers, friends of your family, your friend's parents, church leaders, adults with whom you've done volunteer work, scout leaders or other club leaders are a few ideas. Really any adult outside your family that you have done any kind of work with or for will do.

STOP List possible references.

After you've thought of some folks who might work, you're not finished. You can't just slap their name on an application and be done with it. You need to ask the person if they are willing to be a reference for you. They have a right to say no.

"No, I can't be a reference for you. You're failing my class, tardy seven times, have ten absences and sleep in class when you are here."

If your prospective reference agrees to be a reference, you need to ask them what they are going to say. There are two reasons for wanting to do this. One, you can decide if you really want to use them. What if they don't have anything to say, or worse, what they say is negative? Two, when you ask a reference what they'll say, it makes them think about an answer. When the phone call from the employer happens, they have something in mind and the phone conversation will go smoothly.

You will need the reference's full name (first and last), what they do for a living (homemaker and retired are occupations), their address and phone number. Make sure you ask them for the number at which they can be reached easily.

You will also need the number of years you've known them. Round this number up to one if you haven't known the reference quite a year. For example, a teacher you've had since the beginning of the school year will be rounded to one.

DATE AND SIGN

Date:	9/19/09	Signature:	*Jennie Withers*

Forgetting to date and sign your application is a sure way to get it thrown away. In the adult world, your signature means something. Signing an application signifies you've told the truth, and you give the employer permission to contact your references, thereby considering you for employment.

Some other things you may see on applications:

LANGUAGES

What foreign languages do you speak fluently?	None	Read:	N/A	Write:	N/A

Speaking a foreign language fluently means you can carry on a conversation with a native speaker. It doesn't mean you're taking Spanish II at school. The first is a yes or no question. If the answer is *no*, whether you can read or write the language is not applicable (*N/A*). If the answer is *yes*, then read and write become yes or no questions.

MILITARY SERVICE

U.S. Military or Naval Service:	None	Rank:	N/A	Present Membership in National Guard or Reserves:	None

Military service is going to be *None*. JROTC programs in high school don't count for military service. If they can't send you to war then you are not serving in the military. Rank will therefore be *N/A*, and National Guard membership will be *None*.

PHYSICAL RECORD

Were you ever injured?	No	Give details: N/A		
Have you any defects in hearing?	No	In Vision? No		In Speech? No
In case of emergency notify:	Phyllis Hendrickson	1616 Tam Dr.		(208) 774 - 9087
	Name	Address		Phone

When an employer asks about an injury, they are not asking about the time when you were five and broke your arm. They want to know about current injuries that could affect what you are able to do at work. The reason employers may ask for information about your physical health is because they don't want to cause you further injury.

Having an injury doesn't mean they won't hire you, but it might mean if you have a bad back they won't make you lug around boxes in a warehouse. The questions are yes or no questions. If the answer to the injury question is *no*, then giving details is not applicable (*N/A*).

The emergency contact information should be the name of a parent or guardian, your home address and a phone number where your parent or guardian can be reached. If you are hired, you will fill out this type of information more extensively.

AVAILABILITY

	Monday	Tuesday	Wednesday	Thursday	Friday	Saturday	Sunday
From:		4:00 p.m.		4:00 p.m.			
To:		8:00 p.m.		8:00 p.m.			

Not reliable transportation

Many applications, particularly those for part time positions, will ask you when you are available to work. Be as specific as you can, and don't be afraid to write down times when you cannot work.

There may also be a question about how you plan to get to and from work. Employers want to know that you have a reliable means of transportation.

Some Applications Come with More and More Questions

Many employers like to give a questionnaire with their applications. These applications are usually done on computer, or if they are paper applications, you will not be allowed to take them out of the business. Make sure you plan for enough time to fill out an application and to do a questionnaire if needed.

Basic skills, especially simple math

If a customer gets a sandwich at $5.15, a bag of chips for $.99, and a drink for $1.49, with a tax rate of 6%, what would the customer's total bill be? Employers want to know that if the power goes out, or the register breaks, you have the ability to figure somebody's check.

Interacting with customers and fellow employees

The customer says she asked for no mustard on her sandwich, but you know she did. What do you do? Keep in mind the credo 'the customer is always right' with questions like this. "Make another sandwich" is a good answer.

Your shift is about to end when a customer wants you to see if you can find an item in the other stores in town. What would you do? Of course you want to help the customer, but keep in mind a part-time employee can't work too many hours. If the request will only take a few minutes, then take care of it. If it will be a longer ordeal, then leave the customer in the capable hands of a fellow employee.

Chain of command

The employee who is supposed to come in and relieve you is thirty minutes late, what do you do? If your answer is "stay until somebody shows up", you're wrong. This is a chain of command question. The right answer is to call your manager or shift supervisor and ask them what they want you to do. It is not your decision whether to stay.

You notice that someone you work with spends a lot of time on the phone, meets people in the parking lot where packages are exchanged. You think drugs may be involved, what do you do? **You need to** schedule a time with your manager to tell him/her what's going on. If it turns out to be nothing, then there's no harm done. If it does turn out to be an illegal activity, and you knew about it but did nothing, you could be charged as an accessory. It's also not safe for you to confront the fellow employee about your suspicions.

> *Real integrity is doing the right thing, knowing that nobody's going to know whether you did it or not.*
> *~Oprah Winfrey*

Honesty

The way to test honesty is by asking the same questions in many different ways.

How would you describe your attendance at school? Many businesses and schools require an excuse for absences. If there is no excuse, it is called an unexcused absence. How many unexcused absences have you had from work or school? Sometimes people are late to work or school. How many times have you been late to work or school?

These questions are scattered throughout the questionnaire. It is proven liars aren't consistent, therefore they will answer these questions differently and the employer will know they're lying.

Don't Be a Liar, Liar, Pants on Fire!

Honesty is extremely important on an application. Liars usually get caught. I said usually, so that means there is a chance you won't. Whether you get caught or not isn't the point. You want to be a person of integrity. It's the most important thing you can be. Integrity is the one thing guaranteed to make you feel good about yourself. Without it, you are miserable.

> *Lisa was sixteen, but looked old for her age. She decided to apply for a job as a cocktail waitress. She lied about her age on the application and during the interview in order to get the job. Lisa was hired, but when she put her social security number on her W-4 form, it was immediately discovered she was only sixteen. She was fired before she was finished being hired, and because employers talk, Lisa earned a reputation as a liar.*

Everyone in life has a purpose, even if it's to serve as a bad example

Lisa's social security number outed her as a liar, but there are many ways to check your honesty. You could be asked the same question on the application, in the interview and on a questionnaire. When you are nervous and under pressure it is extremely likely you will be found out if you're not being honest. Honesty really is the best policy. You will have a chance to explain if there's something on your application or the questionnaire that doesn't make you look good.

> *I'm not smart enough to lie.*
> *~Ronald Reagan*

The Internet

The internet is a wonderful thing. Information is readily available. That includes information about you. What would a prospective employer see if they Googled your name? What is on your My Space or Facebook Pages? How about what you've done with Twitter? Do you post video clips on You Tube? Whatever you have out there - your pictures, your words, your videos – are accessible to employers. Don't think they won't check you out online. It just may be the most honest reference available to them. Employers know it and they know how to Google. If there is anything you have on the internet that you would hesitate to show your parents, get it off before you apply for employment!

Treat the application as if it is your one and only shot because, quite frankly, it is. It is not the place to do a good job. It has to be great. Make no mistake; nobody is going to give you a job. You will have to earn one. The application is your first step.

Keys for Filling Out Applications

- If not typed, blue or black ink

- Read the application carefully

- Write neatly, don't use abbreviations

- Don't leave blanks, know the difference between N/A and none

- Find 3 adult references, ask them to be a reference and ask them what they'll say in advance

- Check it over – a lot

- Be prepared for a questionnaire

- Be honest

- Check out what you have out in cyberspace- view it as an employer would

FAQs - All Those Blanks

Can I use a nickname, what I prefer to be called, on an application?
Yes, you can on the application, but when you get the job and fill out the W-4 form, you need to use the name on your birth certificate and your social security card.

What is a letter of reference?
Occasionally, an employer may ask for a letter of reference. A letter of reference is simply a letter written about your work ethic by the people you have asked to be your references. The same rules for choosing these references apply. But, the one thing to remember is that you need to choose people who can write a legible letter for you. Ask the reference if you can have a copy of the letter. They will usually give you one.

Why do I need three references, why can't I have two?
Two may work for some applications, but the business standard is three references. If you only have two on an application asking for three, the employer isn't going to look at it. The standard number to turn in with a résumé is also three.

What if my reference moved out of the area?
If you have no other reference to use then keep them as a reference, but write down their new information.

What if I just moved to the area and don't know anyone to use as a reference?
Use the references you know from where you moved, but you may want to explain your situation when you turn in your application.

Will employers really call my references?
Some do, some don't, but you don't want to take any chances.

What do I do if I have no phone?
Find a reliable friend, neighbor or relative who will get you a message.

What if I worked in my family's business and got paid for my work, can I use it as employment history?
Yes, but try to find someone to put down from the business besides your parent as a contact. Make sure it is still someone who can talk about your work ethic.

What if my employer went out of business, can I use them as work history?
Yes, you can. Make sure you can still contact someone you worked for. On the application for **Reason for Leaving**, you will put *job ended*.

If I left a job because of bad conditions, can I use that as work history?
This is a touchy situation because if you left because you were unhappy, and the employer knew it, they may not say good things about you. If you left without giving two weeks notice, this is a particular concern. Use this job as work history if you managed to leave on good terms with the manager, and you are sure they'll talk positively about you.

What if the application asks about physical defects?
Then answer the question honestly. Employers want to know this information so they can find a suitable placement for you. It's illegal for them to discriminate, so it doesn't mean you won't get hired, but it may affect your placement.

What if an employer requests my grade point average or a transcript?

You can get a transcript or a grade point average from your counselor's office at school. If an employer requests a transcript, ask them if you can bring it in or if they would like the school to send it to them. When the school sends a transcript, it is called an 'official transcript'.

If I turned in an application and I don't hear anything from the employer, can I call?

Yes, you can. When it comes to applications, the employer is not obligated to call you if you didn't get an interview. But, if you are curious, give them a week and then call. Politely tell them who you are, that you turned in an application recently and you were wondering if they filled the position. You can also request that the employer keep your application on file for future openings. If they agree, you need to call when another opening arises and remind the employer they have your application and that you would like them to look at it.

SAMPLE APPLICATION

PERSONAL INFORMATION

NAME: _____

| | last | first | middle |

ADDRESS: _____

| | street | city | state |

PHONE :

REFERRED BY:

EMPLOYMENT DESIRED

| Position | Date you can start | Salary desired |

EDUCATION

Type of School	Name of School City, State	Date Attended	Graduate	Degree and Major Field(s) of Study
High School			Yes ( ) No ( )	
College			Yes ( ) No ( )	
Other			Yes ( ) No ( )	

SPECIAL SKILLS, TRAINING, OR ACTIVITIES

| |
| |
| |
| |

| What foreign languages do you speak fluently? | Read | Write |
| U.S. Military or Naval Service | Rank | Present Membership in National Guard or Reserves |

PHYSICAL RECORD

Were you ever injured?	Give details:	
Have you any defects in hearing?	In Vision?	In Speech?
In case of emergency notify		
Name	Address	Phone

EMPLOYMENT HISTORY

Date	Name, address and phone number of employer	Position	Salary	Reason for Leaving
From				
To				

Date	Name, address and phone number of employer	Position	Salary	Reason for Leaving
From				
To				

REFERENCES

Name and occupation	Address	Phone Number	Years Known

I authorize investigation of all statements contained in this application. I understand that misrepresentation or omission of facts called on is cause for dismissal. Further, I understand and agree that my employment is for no definite period and may, regardless of the date of payment of my wages and salary, be terminated at any time without previous notice.

Date _____   Signature _____

Notes

Notes

Section 3: *Don't Panic, It's Just a Résumé*

Hey, Get a Job!

The Résumé

A résumé is defined as a written document that lists your work experience, skills and educational background. Many of my students believe there is no possible way they could write a résumé because they have nothing to put on it. By definition, however, teens have two of the three parts. Even if you don't have work history, you do have skills and educational background.

It is true that few employers will ask to see a résumé for entry level jobs. But it is also true that if you want to apply for better jobs offering more money, they will require a résumé. In other words if you plan on getting more than one job in your lifetime, then you will have to know how to write a résumé. It is a good idea to learn how to write a résumé now and then add to it as your work experience, skill set and education evolve.

Résumés are not only used for employment. College and scholarship applications may also call for a résumé. It is also a common practice for teachers to request a résumé when asked to write a letter of recommendation. A résumé provides a brief summary of where a student has been, and where they are going.

In this section I will provide the do's and don'ts of résumé writing as well as examples that lend themselves to teens who have very little or no work experience. The example résumés are very basic and you can create one on www.heygetajob.com . After you've created a basic résumé, you can choose to copy and paste the information into a template. There are good templates on http://office.microsoft.com/en-us/templates and a number of other websites. Most templates will allow you to change the headings if you need to, but doing a search for 'entry level résumé should give you something that doesn't require a lot of changes.

NOT A GOOD RÉSUMÉ!!!

The example was turned in by one of my students; before he had my class of course. He couldn't figure out why he didn't get the job.

Résumé Basics

Résumés must be typed.
Use a business type font like Times New Roman, Tacoma or Arial. The size can be less, but not more than 12. Templates will have a set font. Don't be tempted to change it.

Print résumés on a high quality paper.
This means higher quality paper than you'll find in a school or library printer. If you visit any office supply store they will sell paper specifically for résumés. You should notice that résumé paper doesn't come in a rainbow of colors. What colors there are (usually white, cream and gray) are very muted. Your finished product should look clean and professional.

Keep your résumé to one page.
It is a brief document to sell you as a qualified candidate. And let's face it, you haven't lived long enough and had enough experience to go over one page. If it's too long, employers won't take the time.

> Jason White
> 1111 N. Orchard
> Boise, Id. 83705
> (208) 888-0009
>
> **I LIKE TO WATCH MOVIES AND PLAY VIDEO GAMES SO I THINK MY FIRST JOB SHOULD BE AT STAR VIDEO.**
> **THANK YOU FOR YOUR TIME.**

Use a proper format.

You can create a basic résumé on my website www.heygetajob.com . If you want to jazz it up a bit, try a Microsoft Office template or one of the many templates available on the internet. Don't try and reinvent the wheel, so-to-speak. Choose a résumé format that allows the reader to easily scan your résumé, and one that highlights your strengths.

Write in the active voice.

A bad (passive) example: I have written technical manuals for company procedures. A good (active) example: I wrote technical manuals for company procedures. An easy way to write in the active voice is to start statements with a verb. For example: Created a filing system for daycare records.

Focus on these three skills: communication skills, problem solving skills, and technical skills.

You should be able to discuss these skills with or without work experience. Communication skills are those traits that enable you to get along with other people and work within a team. It includes verbal and written communication. Problem solving simply means you can identify a problem, develop solutions to the problem and make effective decisions to solve the problem in a timely manner. Technical skills refer to your ability to use computers and other digital devices.

> *If you call failures experiments, you can put them in your résumé and claim them as achievements.*
> *~Mason Cooley*

Pay attention to words.

You want words that will grab the attention of the reader. Here is a list of fifty words to give you an idea of what I mean.

assisted	implemented	received
accomplished	improved	recommended
contributed	mediated	represented
coordinated	motivated	revised
created	negotiated	selected
developed	operated	strengthened
designed	organized	structured
defined	oversaw	suggested
earned	participated	supervised
evaluated	performed	taught
examined	planned	trained
facilitated	prepared	transformed
fulfilled	presented	upgraded
generated	published	utilized
headed	pursued	validated
identified		wrote

I'm sure you can probably come up with many more. The point is to make you sound action oriented.

 Make a list of the things you've done using these words.

Tell the truth.

Don't lie, or even exaggerate on your résumé. Your fabrications may get you an interview, but it will become apparent to the employer during the interview that you were not honest.

You need to have references.

Your references are not written on a résumé like they are on an application, but you need to have them available for the employer. All the same reference rules apply – they must be adults, you must ask them and they need to say nice things about your work ethic. At the bottom of your résumé it will say: *References available upon request*.

Customize your résumé to fit the position for which you are applying.

Résumés really are not a one size fits all. Depending on the job or other purpose like a scholarship application, you will want to tweak your résumé in order to focus on the recruiter's needs.

Check, check and double-check.

Don't depend on spell check, grammar check or just you to edit your résumé. Like the application, a résumé may be your one and only shot at an interview.

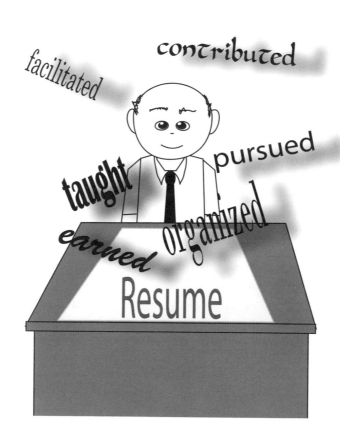

Résumé Worksheet

The following worksheet will take you through what needs to go on your résumé. To create a basic résumé electronically, go to www.heygetajob.com, click on the résumé link and input the information there.

The items with an asterisk * are required. Items without an asterisk are optional. As you will see, you will want to fill in as much as you can. Otherwise, your résumé is going to be very sparse. Once you have your information, look at the example résumés to determine the order you would like the information to appear. If there is not enough room here, use the Notes pages at the end of the section.

*Contact Information

Name	
Address	
City, State, Zip Code	
Phone number (where you can easily be reached)	
email address	

*Objective – One sentence that states why you are sending your résumé to them. You can also use the objective to state the strengths you can contribute to the position.

×Education

Name of your school	
Grade Level	
GPA (only if you are an above average student)	
Names of challenging courses you have taken or those that would help you in a particular job	

Work Experience – Begin with your most recent job first and work your way back. As with the application, if you are still working there, write *present*. If you have more than one past job, use the Notes pages at the end of the chapter.

Date started – Date ended	
Position title	
Company Name	

List of your duties (remember use active voice)

Volunteer or community service experience – This section will look like the Work Experience section and include the same information.

Date started – Date ended	
Title or Role	
Organization Name	

List of your duties (remember use active voice)

Talents or skills that would be relevant to the position

Honors and awards (academic, athletic, community)

*Extracurricular activities – clubs, associations, activities outside of school, hobbies and interests

You can choose a template to jazz-up a résumé, but the key is to demonstrate why you should be hired. If you don't have enough to create at least a ¾ page résumé then there might be a problem. Work on building skills with the classes you take at school, begin some volunteer work and try to join a club or participate in an extracurricular activity. In short, get involved. Even if you don't need a résumé now, you will in the near future. Give yourself some things to work with.

> *One of the signs of passing youth is the birth of a sense of fellowship with other human beings as we take our place among them.*
>
> *Virginia Woolf*

Cover Letter

Once you've completed a résumé, you are not yet finished. A cover letter should accompany your résumé. It is another way to sell yourself as an employee, and sometimes your most powerful method of setting yourself apart from the competition. A cover letter is your formal introduction to the employer. You can put your personality into the cover letter, tell the employer why you want the position, highlight your best skills and let the employer know you are a professional who can write well. See the example at the end of this section.

Questions your cover letter should answer:

- Why are you applying for the job?
- Why did you choose that particular place to apply?
- What are the skills and characteristics you possess that make you a good fit for the job?

Cover Letter Basics

One page or less.
If the cover letter is too long it indicates to the employer that it's full of fluff and the employer won't read it.

Standard business letter format.
It needs to be typed in a business format. Formatting can easily be done in Word. The paper it's written on should match the paper of the résumé.

Have someone else edit for you.
This is an introduction and you may not get another chance. It's not enough to edit yourself. We have a tendency to miss errors in our own work.

Make sure your cover letter is appropriate for the audience.
You will not send the same cover letter to an employer that you would a scholarship committee. Like the résumé, the cover letter is not a one size fits all.

Focus on what you can bring to the job.
Tell them why they should pick you over someone else. After reading your letter, you want the employer to see what makes you different, better than other candidates.

Submitting Your Application Materials

Today, many employers and all job search websites will require you to submit your application, résumé and cover letter online. Here are some things to be aware of:

- **Many sites will require you to create a login and password in order to submit.** Be sure to write them down so you can access the site at a later date.

- **Some programs will require you to type in or copy and paste your résumé into predefined fields.** The fields provided may not correlate exactly to the information that you would like to convey. For example, the fields provided may only ask about previous work history, but you had planned to relate your experience from a volunteer project. There is no **Other** or **Skills** fields provided. You will need to read all fields carefully and be creative in including the information, like putting your volunteer experience in work history.

- **Programs that allow you to upload your résumé will often ignore or distort all your carefully chosen fonts, graphics and formatting.** The only way to eliminate the problem completely is to upload in a read-only file type such as PDF. If these are not accepted, some ways to minimize the problem include:

  o Keep formatting to a minimum (indents, bullets, etc.)
  o Use only standard fonts (Arial, Times New Roman)
  o Eliminate graphics

- **Regardless of what precautions you take, be prepared to spend some time proofing and editing once your upload is complete.** Keep in mind that most upload programs do not have spell check!

One of the disadvantages of submitting your application materials online is that it allows employers to screen applicants without ever meeting them in person. You have very few chances to make an impression on a potential employer, and it is very difficult to do that through résumés and applications. Whenever possible, you should submit your materials in person and ask to deliver to HR or the hiring manager rather than leaving with a receptionist or someone else.

SAMPLE COVER LETTER

1414 Canyon Way
Challis, ID 87707

April 30, 2009

Mr. E. Forester
Human Resources
Hard Workers, Inc.
587 E. Labor Way
Twin Falls, ID 45678

Dear Mr. Forester,

I am interested in your advertisement for a technician's assistant. I have completed the second year of the computer technology program at the Professional Technical Center in Boise, Idaho. My goal after high school is to become a computer engineer. I would appreciate a chance to learn from your technicians.

I am available for a part time position. I can start working as soon as possible. I believe I would be a perfect technician's assistant. I am adept with computers and computer accessories. I have gone through extensive training and would like to put that training to work. I have a positive attitude, know how to work within a team and look forward to learning new computer applications.

Thank you for your time and consideration. You can reach me on my cell phone, 208-890-4727, or my email, computerace@network.com .

Sincerely,

Mark Smith

Mark Smith

As you can see from the example, cover letters don't need to be lengthy. Think of it as an introduction to your résumé, yourself and your goals as they pertain to the job for which you are applying . If you are applying for a scholarship or to a college, the cover letter will serve the same purpose. Instead of discussing a job you will write about what you will bring to a certain college or how a scholarship could help you reach your goals.

A résumé and cover letter should not be feared, but they should be taken seriously. If an employer asks for a résumé that is your application. Therefore, the same amount of care needs to be taken with a cover letter and résumé that should be taken with an application.

Keys for Résumés

- The résumé should look clean and professional

- Keep it to a page

- Write in the active voice

- Focus on problem solving, communication and technical abilities

- Be honest

- Go to www.heygetajob.com to set up a basic résumé

- Use online templates to jazz up your résumé

- Be prepared with needed information for three references

- Have someone else edit for you

- Create a cover letter to introduce your résumé

- Make changes to your résumé to fit the audience

Keys for Cover Letters

- Keep it to one page or less

- Write in standard business letter format

- Focus on why you are applying for the job, how it fits into your goals and important characteristics you can bring

- Have someone else edit for you

- Make changes to your cover letter to fit the audience

FAQs – Don't Panic, It's Just a Résumé

What if I don't have a computer at home to do a résumé?
Your school or public library has computers that you can use, and most of them will have internet and/or Word. If you can get to www.heygetajob.com you can do a résumé. They may print for you, but plan on a small charge for doing so. If you can't print, take your saved résumé to a printing business like Kinkos or an office supply store with printing capabilities.

If I turned in a résumé and I don't hear anything from the employer, can I call?
Yes, you can. As with applications, the employer is not obligated to call you if you didn't get an interview. But, if you are curious, give them a week and then call.

If I turned in a résumé for something besides a job and I didn't hear back, can I call?
Yes, you can. There should be information about when the applicants can expect to hear from them. Make sure that date has passed before you call.

Does my résumé have to be a full page?
No. Obviously you want it to look like it has substance, but you also don't want to force the issue. Don't try to add unnecessary words like very, use larger font sizes and have too much white space. Employers will pick up on those things just like your English teacher does. If you don't have enough to make about ¾ a page, you should look into what you need to add to your life in order to do that.

What if the template I want to use doesn't have the right headings?
Change them. Most templates, especially those from Microsoft, give you the capability to change all aspects of the template.

What if I don't know how to write a business letter?
Microsoft Word has business letter templates built into it. If you can't use Word, then type 'business letter' into a search engine and use the results to guide you.

Example 1 - This résumé highlights practical experience having to do with the desired job. Notice it isn't work experience, but it is every bit as valuable.

JACK FISHER

1477 Redwood Dr.
Kuna, ID 88101
jack.fisher@needajob.com
(208) 505-1388

OBJECTIVE
To experience the day-to-day operations of a publishing firm through a part-time job or summer internship.

EDUCATION
Completed three years at Kuna High School.
Graduation date: May 2011.
G.P.A. 3.75.

EXPERIENCE
Newspaper Staff, Kuna High School

- **Aug 2008 - present.** Editor of school newspaper.
- **Aug 2008 - present.** Researched for articles using library and Web sources. Composed and edited articles, columns and editorials. Worked with newspaper layout and publishing software.

Yearbook Staff, Kuna High School

- **Aug 2008 - present.** Leader of design team from layout through finished product.

RELEVANT HIGH SCHOOL STUDIES
Technical writing; advanced composition; marketing; business; video production; computer classes-word processing, publishing, troubleshooting and fixing minor computer problems.

HONORS, AWARDS, AND MEMBERSHIPS

- **2009 High School Newspaper Design winner**
  Idaho State Journalist's Conference, sponsored by Boise State University.
- **Member of high school chapter of**
  Business Professionals of America (BPA), 2008 - present
- **Treasurer of National Honor Society, 2008 - present**

References available upon request.

Example 2 - This résumé is another example of organizing information when you don't have work experience, but you do have some useful skills to offer.

Denise Taylor
1630 Mountain View, Helena, MT 67890
510-780-1302
dtaylor@wantajob.com

OBJECTIVE

Organized and dependable teen looking for an opportunity to gain work experience through a part time job.

EXPERIENCE AND ACCOMPLISHMENTS

Problem-solving skills

- Librarian aide at Helena High School where I resolved computer issues and invented a system to retrieve overdue books.

Organizational skills

- Awarded "Library Aide of the Year 2009" for organizational skills.
- Reorganized computer tracking of the library books.
- Organized various events for lunchtime activities in the library.

Technology skills

- Earned "A" in all computer classes.
- Built personal computer from scratch.
- Can type 70 words per minute.

VOLUNTEER HISTORY

Helena Food Bank — Summer 2008, Summer 2009

Helena, Montana
Organize and inventory food bank items

SCHOOL ORGANIZATIONS

Helena High Key Club — 2008 - 2009
Vice-president — 2009

Helena High School Women's Basketball Team — 2008 - 2009
Team member

EDUCATION

Helena High School
2008 - 2009
Graduation Date: 2012

References available upon request.

Example 3 - This résumé includes work experience as well as volunteer work.

Jordan Chase
123 Sunny Lane
Sun Valley, ID 98562
(208) 455-2461 — Jordan@getajob.com

Objective

Mature and responsible high school senior interested in the dental field seeking a part-time position at a dentist's office.

Work Experience

Roaring Springs
Summer 2008 and 2009
Lifeguard

- Monitored swimming areas for rule violations and swimmers in trouble.
- Assisted with pool and park maintenance.
- Supervised children's events and parties.
- Attended training courses and maintained CPR certification.
- Taught summer swimming classes.

Allred Construction
Fall 2008 - Spring 2009

- Picked-up and delivered supplies for construction jobs.
- Preparing bills and advertisements to be sent.
- Filing and organizing job information.
- Answered phone and delivered messages.
- Scheduled estimates for construction supervisors.

Volunteer Work

Big Brothers/Big Sisters
2008 - 2009

- Assisted with and participated in group activities and field trips.
- Tutored ages 8-13 and assisted with homework assignments.

School Organizations

Student Council Representative
2008-2009 School Year

Education

Sun Valley High School
2006 - 2009
May 2010 Graduation

References available upon request.

Notes

Notes

Section 4: *I'm Speechless*

Hey, Get a Job!

You turned in the perfect application and the employer calls for an interview. You are immediately and painfully nervous. It's normal to feel this way. Even adults who have had many interviews get nervous for them. In fact, there is something wrong with the person who doesn't get nervous. Having said that, a little nerves are good, but paralyzing nervousness is not. You can avoid paralysis by preparing for the interview.

Tips for an Interview

Appearance is key to a good interview.

It needs to be absolutely understood that employers do not care about your freedom of expression, your personal style. Dress conservatively for the interview; be clean and neat in your appearance. Employers know nothing about you, so your appearance is going to mean a lot. Their objective is to hire people that are going to make them look good. If you appear dirty or weird (society's definition, not yours), you won't get the job.

Cleverly disguised as responsible adults.

I'm not saying you need to wear church clothes to the interview, but you need to look respectable. With today's styles, there are a few things you should know. **For guys, pull up your pants! Nobody really wants to see your underwear, no matter how cool you think it may look. For girls, cover up the three B's which are: butt, belly and boobs!** And believe it or not, tattoos, piercings, and heavy make-up are not going to help you get a job either.

> *Adam filled out the perfect application for a department store. He dressed neatly and was clean for his interview. He brushed his shoulder length hair until it shone. He prepared for the questions that may be asked in an interview. He showed up early and spit out his gum. The interview went off without a hitch. At the end, the employer said to Adam, "I would love to hire you, but I can't. We have a dress code here, and I'm afraid your hair is too long. I'm sorry, but unless you cut your hair, I won't hire you." Adam needed and wanted that job. He cut his hair.*

I know of few businesses that don't have some sort of requirements for appearance and dress. You may have to take a look at your priorities. Is it more important for you to look and dress a certain way, or have a job?

Arrive early for your interview.

Getting there five to ten minutes early says to an employer that you are punctual, which is important to them. Pretend you are a member of the New York Giants football team. Their coach tells them unless they're five minutes early to a meeting, they are late.

Body language is the majority of communication.

When meeting the employer, smile and make eye contact. Shake hands firmly, do not give them the fish or dead hand. It is a sign of weakness in our culture. Girls, that includes you. Stand or sit straight, maintain a good posture. In other words, don't sit like you do in the desks at school, all slumped with your legs stretched out in front of you.

> *It takes seventy-two muscles to frown, but only thirteen to smile.*
> *~Unknown*

My theory is that if you look confident you can pull off anything-even if you have no clue what you're doing.
~Jessica Alba

Communicate confidence in yourself.

One of the hardest things for human beings to do is to talk positively about themselves. Maybe it's because we are taught from an early age not to brag. It's not bragging to convince an employer your personality and talents are what they need. It is imperative that you talk about what you, as an individual, can bring to a job. If you have a difficult time talking yourself up, ask a parent or a good friend.

Listen carefully.

Let the interviewer start the dialogue. Make sure you are listening to what he/she is asking so you can answer appropriately.

Be prepared, but not rehearsed.

Yes you can prepare for an interview, but preparing doesn't mean you memorize a set of answers. If memorized, it will sound rehearsed, which sounds fake.

You are going to have to talk.

Although answers don't have to be five minutes long, they do need to be more than one word, even more than a few sentences. If you are not prepared to speak at length with your interviewer, it is going to be an awkward experience.

Common Interview Questions and Tips on How to Answer Them

Obviously I can't tell you exactly what the interviewer will ask, but there are types of questions that are very common. Besides, all interview questions are essentially asking the same question: WHY SHOULD I HIRE YOU?

Tell me about yourself.

This is a common ice breaker question, but it is still an interview question with a specific purpose. Talk about you as a worker. Some good adjectives to use:

responsible	determined	hard working
diligent	trustworthy	team-player
motivated	reliable	self starter
loyal	intelligent	attentive
conscientious	industrious	persistent
dynamic	energetic	enthusiastic
assertive	consistent	organized
punctual	fast learner	leader
independent	mature	social
honest	self-confident	dependable

There are many more, but before you use them make sure you know what the word means, and that it describes you.

Why are you interested in working here? or **How do you think you will fit into this operation?**
Do your research to prepare for this type of question. Before you can talk about why you want the job or how you'll fit in, you need to know what they do and how they operate. Even if you think you know, look it up to make sure. Find some positive things about the business, and then figure out how those things fit in with your goals. Do not include your need for money. We all need money so you don't want to state the obvious. Your goal in answering this question is to assure the employer that you are mature enough to know the world doesn't revolve around you and your wants and immediate needs.

> *While preparing for her interview, Anita found that McDonald's promotes teamwork. She also discovered McDonald's has a scholarship program for their employees. One of Anita's goals was to attend college, and as a people person, she loved the idea of being part of a team. She discussed these things in her interview. She not only got the job, but Anita is currently attending college by way of scholarship from McDonald's.*

If you do some research and find that nothing interests you, then you might want to reconsider working there.

What is your major weakness?
Believe it or not, by the time you're finished answering this question, you should no longer have a weakness in the mind of your employer. You can do this two ways. One is to talk about a weakness that really isn't a weakness. For example, my answer to this question was that I tend to over plan. This is a positive trait in the world of teaching when you have to be able to adjust lessons on the fly according the needs of your students. The second way is to talk about a weakness, but then discuss how you are overcoming it. Either way, it is key that you end the conversation on a positive.

> *Brent had difficulty getting to class on time. When he started applying for jobs, he realized how important arriving on time is to employers. Brent changed his ways at school. He made an effort and started arriving on time. When he was asked about his weakness in an interview, he said, "Well, my weakness would be punctuality. I used to get a lot of tardies at school, but in the last two months I have made a real effort to change that. I haven't gotten a single tardy in over a month and a half."*

What are your strengths? or **How do others describe you?**

My strength is I can bench 200 pounds.

Tell the employer what attributes you have that will make you a good employee. The answer may sound very similar to the "tell me about yourself" question, but this should be more in depth. The adjectives listed earlier would still apply, but you need to give examples or proof as to why they describe you. For example, if you say you're intelligent, throwing in your stellar GPA would be a good idea. If you say you're a hard worker, telling them about helping your family with a project would validate the statement. Again, if you have a hard time talking about yourself, ask a parent or friend how they would describe your strengths.

Give an example of how you solved a problem in the past. or Give an example where you showed leadership. or Give an example when you contributed to a team.
These questions are all asking for situations where you used problem solving skills and got something done. It doesn't have to be a 'how I saved the world' kind of example. It can be an everyday thing where you proved you have the intelligence, initiative and work ethic to get something done. Think about times when you were part of a team or group to complete something like a school project or an important game or season. Maybe it could be an example when you acted as a mediator (stay away from romantic issues), or had to communicate with adults in order to achieve a goal.

Do you have any questions for me?

At the end of all interviews, the employer will ask, "Do you have any questions for me?" Having a question for the employer demonstrates you are interested in the business, and you really want the job. Try to come up with one. Again, the research you do on the place of business should help with this. If nothing comes up, then ask questions about the position for which you are applying -

   What would my specific duties be?
   What days or hours can I expect to work?
   How do I advance within the company?
   Are you willing to work with extracurricular schedules?
These types of questions are all good choices. Just remember to ask tactful questions that show you are interested in the job, and you are ready to be a good employee. Remember, questions about how much you're going to get paid are not tactful questions.

 List words that describe you, your weaknesses, problems you've solved and when you've lead and contributed to a team.

How important is it to prepare?
Less than 20% of applications received lead to job interviews. Less than ½ of that 20% are hired.

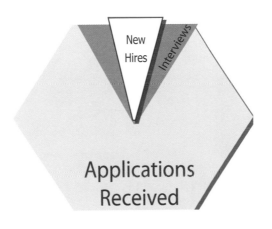

Keys for Interviewing

- Appearance – employers hire people who make them, and their business look good

- Arrive early

- Use body language to communicate self-confidence

- Don't be afraid to speak positively about yourself

- Listen carefully to the employer

- Prepare, prepare, prepare

FAQs - I'm Speechless

What if the interviewer does not reach out to shake my hand?

Don't take it personally. Some people have a problem with shaking another's hand. Don't force the issue. Always take your cue from the employer.

Can I be funny, peppy or boring during the interview?

Yes, it's o.k. to show your personality, whatever that may be. However, you do need to provide serious answers to questions.

Can I be interviewed when I turn in my application?

Yes, an employer can ask for an interview right then. It's not common, but it could happen. You can prepare in advance for that request, or you can simply ask the employer if you can schedule an interview at a later time.

Should I tell an employer the days and times I can and cannot work?

YES! You need to be up front about that information during the interview, especially if it wasn't on the application. Employers realize you have other commitments besides work. What will be irritating for an employer is if they hire you planning that you will work a certain time and you can't.

How many days does it take for an employer to call me after an interview?

Employers should call and let you know whether or not you got the job after an interview. If you have not heard within a week whether you've been hired or passed over, then call and ask. Respectfully remind them who you are and when you interviewed and tell them you didn't hear back from them. If you didn't get the job, ask them, respectfully of course, why you didn't get it. Tell them you are new at the process and would like to know how you can be better next time. That way it wasn't a wasted experience.

Notes

Notes

Section 5: *So Now I Work, Right? Wrong!*

Hey, Get a Job!

You got hired! It's very exciting and you can't wait to get started. There's only one thing standing in your way: the hiring packet. Once you've been hired, the employer will give you a packet or a website with many wonderful things for you to fill out, read and learn before you start your new job. Of course, not all hiring packets are going to be exactly the same, but the following is common:

W-4 forms.

All employees must fill out a W-4 form. The W-4's purpose is so your employer can withhold the correct federal income tax from your pay. You will probably not have to have any money taken out for federal income tax because you are a dependent, meaning your parents take a deduction for you on their income taxes. This is called being exempt. To declare exemption on the W-4, you will complete only lines 1, 2, 3, 4, and 7 and sign the form. Beware of the employer with a licensed business who wants to pay you under the table. Under the table means there are no taxes or other government monies taken out of your check. This could result in your having to file taxes as a small business. In essence, you're taking on part of your employer's tax burden. You don't want that. See W-4 at the end of this section.

> *There's nothing wrong with the younger generation that becoming taxpayers won't cure.*
>
> *~ Dan Bennett*

"I want my mommy!"

Your social security number has to be on the W-4.

You need to have it, or you can't be hired.

Emergency Contact Sheet.

In case something happens to you at work, employers need to have emergency contacts on file. You will need to have the names and phone numbers (home, work, and cell) for parents or guardians and a friend of the family. Throughout your employment, if any of this information changes, you need to update this card.

> *Tia worked for a fast food restaurant. One night at work, she had an accident with the fryer. The hot grease burned her hand and arm quite badly. An ambulance was called to take her to the emergency room. Her employer pulled her emergency card, but found the numbers she wrote down for her parents were no longer in service. Tia forgot to update the card when her parents divorced. Tia spent a lonely, and very scary, two hours in the emergency room before anybody was able to track down her parents.*

Employment Eligibility.

This is the form that proves you are a U.S. citizen, or are able to work legally in the United States. You will need to fill out the personal information and provide one document from List A, or one document from both List B and List C. See the following link for more information: http://www.uscis.gov/files/form/I-9.pdf.

Company Policies.

This part of your hire packet will vary by company, but again, there are going to be a few items that are standard. Rules you must follow at work, training materials, operations (like payroll) are things found in this portion.

Training Materials.
You are going to have to read and maybe even study and test on some things before you are eligible to start work.

> *Alison got a job working in a paint store. She was given a large binder of information on the products she would be selling and safety information for handling hazardous materials. When Alison felt she knew a section of this information, she took a test on it. Although she did get paid for the time she spent in the office, Alison had to do much of the studying at home and was not paid for this study time. She was required to receive an 80% or better on all tests before she could start the job for which she was hired.*

Like anything in life, education is necessary. Even if your job seems like it should be easy, there will be training involved.

Rules to be followed, including dress code.
All businesses have a set of rules for employees to follow. If you don't, you won't be working for them. Many of the policies schools have are in place because the adult world of work wants young people to get into the habit of dressing and acting appropriately, being there, being there on time, working within a group or team, and meeting deadlines. The same things that are expected of you at school will be expected of you at work. Only more so. Remember Life Rule # 4 – If you think your teacher is tough; wait till you get a boss.

Clothes make the man. Naked people have little or no influence on society.
~Mark Twain

Unless you wear a uniform to school, you will have to get used to a stricter dress code at work. No matter what job you get, there will be standards for your appearance and for your safety on the job. It could be the length of your hair, the shoes you wear or a complete uniform that has to be worn to work. When you accept the job, you accept the dress code. The dress code will be in the hiring packet or the boss will tell you what you need to wear. If you are in doubt, ask! A good rule of thumb is to dress up on your first day and observe what other employees are wearing.

Technology is a great thing, but there are those who take advantage of this great thing while they are at work. Therefore, there are rules. Some of these rules may be in a hiring packet, others you are expected to know. Here are some examples:

- No cell phones on the job - this means no calls, no checking messages, no texting

- No IPODS or MP3 players

- No using the company computer for personal e-mails, games, instant messaging or surfing the web

Businesses nationwide know how much time (which translates to dollars for them) employees waste on the items listed above when they should be working. Some companies monitor these things very closely. Remember, when you are being paid to work or are using company equipment, you have no right to privacy. The employer has the right to see what you are doing and to fire you for it.

Harassment Policy.

This will be a part of your hiring packet. It is such a huge issue that it's part of all companies' rules. It is extremely important you understand what constitutes harassment so you can avoid doing it, and you also know if you are a victim. Some of the things you may participate in at school will not fly in the work place.

Defining Harassment -

An incident of offensive comments or conduct involving unwelcome remarks, jokes or slurs, or other verbal or physical conduct, which is known or should reasonably be known to be unwelcome.

A sexual advance or solicitation made by a person who uses his/her authority to threaten with loss of job or anything to do with the job.

A threat for having participated in an investigation of harassment, or for the rejection of sexual solicitation or advance.

Examples of Harassing Behaviors –

- Touching (that includes hitting)

- Verbal comments (teasing, put downs, etc.)

- Name calling

- Spreading sexual rumors

- Sexting

- Leers and stares

- Sexual or "dirty" jokes, cartoons, pictures, and pornography

- Using the computer or electronic devices to leave sexual messages (including forwarding offensive jokes)

- Using the computer or electronic devices to threaten others (emails, MySpace, Facebook, Twitter, texting)

- Gestures with the hands and body

- Pressure for sexual activity

- Cornering, blocking, standing too close

- Conversations that are too personal

- "Rating" an individual

- Obscene t-shirts, hats, pins

- Sexual assault and attempting sexual assault

- Massaging the neck or shoulders

- Touching oneself sexually in front of others

> *Dan loved his job at a family fun center and felt very comfortable with his fellow employees, especially the guys. Dan and his work friends would talk suggestively and rate the female customers that came in. They paid no attention to the other employees who were not participating in their fun. A fellow employee finally got so uncomfortable with their behaviors, Dan and his friends were turned in to management.*
>
> *Dan, and his buddies, were fired.*

- Graffiti

- Making kissing sounds or licking lips suggestively

- Howling, catcalls, whistles

- Repeatedly asking someone out

- Pulling down someone's pants

- Public displays of affection

- Using terms such as 'gay' or 'Jewish' etc. in a derogatory way.

Some of the things we do, or have done to us, never struck us as being harassing behaviors, but they are. Pretty much any behavior that has the possibility to make anyone uncomfortable falls under harassment. You have to be careful about what you say and do; don't assume everyone is o.k. with your behavior. For example, one of my biggest pet peeves is anyone who uses words like 'gay' or 'Jewish' in a derogatory way. It makes the user sound incredibly ignorant, and I am offended and bothered by these terms. Therefore, my rights are violated and I can take legal action.

Everyone has the right to be comfortable at work or school, including you. Just because you are young, doesn't mean you don't have the right to be comfortable at work. If you feel uncomfortable because of harassment, you need to talk to your boss. If your boss is the one making you uncomfortable, talk to your parents or a trusted adult.

When it comes to examples of being a victim of harassment, I don't have examples from a workplace. Unfortunately, I have plenty of examples as a teacher. James was a bully in my school. He picked out those students who were quiet and shy because he believed they would never tell on him. James would say inappropriate things to his victims, spread malicious rumors about them, physically abuse them and recruit his friends to participate as well. James' victims (and there were many) finally had enough. They realized that people who harass will not stop. In fact, their behaviors will only escalate. Some of James' targets had endured James since elementary school. They went to the school counselor and submitted written statements. The last time I saw James was in the Vice Principal's office with a police officer. James' case went to court and he has not been seen in our school since.

Reading Your Paycheck

This should be easy right? You work for 6 hours at $7.00/ hour, so that's $42.00. Wrong! Forty two dollars is your Gross Pay: the amount of the check before the government takes their share. Net Pay is the amount of take home pay (what you get) after deductions are taken out. Most checks are split into two parts: the actual check that you can cash and the stub which tells you where some of your money went. Some common things to see on your check stub:

BEST JOB EVER, INC.			EMPLOYEE	JONATHAN R. DOE	
			SSN	123-45-6789	
PAYROLL ACCOUNT			PAY PERIOD	3/4/09-3/15/09	
			PAY DATE	3/15/09	NET PAY $309.60
			CHECK NO.	06012	

EARNINGS			TAXES WITHHELD		
DESCRIPTION	HRS	AMOUNT	TAX	CURRENT	YTD
REGULAR	40	400.00	FEDERAL TAX	51.80	153.60
OVERTIME			SOCIAL SEC.	24.80	65.10
			MEDICARE	5.80	15.25
			STATE TAX	8.00	31.50
CURRENT		400.00			
YEAR TO DATE		1050.00			

Rate: the hourly rate you are paid

Hours: the number of hours for which you are being paid

Period: the amount you were given for the current pay period

Year to date: how much you've earned (or paid for a certain tax depending on where it appears on the check) for the year thus far

Gross pay: the total amount you earned before deductions

Net pay: the amount of your take home pay

Federal Tax (FW or FTW) – the tax taken out by the federal government – this amount depends on the exemptions written on your W-4

State Tax (ST or SWT) – the tax taken out by the state in which you live

Social Security (SS, FICA or SWT) - Social Security tax withheld – you will pay this tax. This is a required retirement plan.

Medicare Tax (MWT or MED) – Medicare is medical insurance for those over the age of 65.

Other Paycheck Tips –

- If you have any questions, ask! It's your money.

- Check it over – check the calculations, the withholding (the employer is taking out too much or too little according to your exemptions on the W-4), hours worked and address. Keep in mind that if something is incorrect, it may appear on every check.

- Do not use check cashing businesses; they charge higher fees for their services. If you haven't opened a checking and savings account at a bank, you need to. For teens, first time checking and savings accounts are usually free, particularly if your parents bank at the same institution.

The Hiring Packet Keys

• The W-4 form needs to be done the right way. You don't want more money taken out of your check than needed. Your social security number has to be on this form.

• The emergency contact sheet has to have phone numbers that are current and are numbers where someone can be reached.

• The employment eligibility form proves you can work in the country legally. Make sure you bring the forms of ID necessary.

• Know the rules, every business has them. Pay particular attention to harassment.

• You have to know how to do your job. There will be training.

• Know how to read a paycheck.

• Open a checking and savings account at a bank or credit union. It's a good idea to use the same institution your parents do.

SOCIAL SECURITY

000-00-0000

Jennie Withers

Jennie Withers
SIGNATURE

FAQs - So Now I Work, Right? Wrong!

What if I don't know my Social Security number?

Then learn it. You don't want to carry a Social Security card with you. That number is the most important one you have. If you want to prevent identity theft, have the number in your head only.

What if I don't have a Social Security card?

If you have never seen your Social Security card, ask a parent. You were issued a Social Security number at birth. If your parents don't know what happened to it, you will need to contact your local social security office. You can't be employed without a Social Security number.

What if I am emancipated?

First of all, emancipation is not legal in all states, so check that out first. If you are legally emancipated, your parents cannot claim you on their taxes. Therefore, when you fill out your W-4 form, you will fill it out as a single adult.

Form W-4 (2009)

Purpose. Complete Form W-4 so that your employer can withhold the correct federal income tax from your pay. Consider completing a new Form W-4 each year and when your personal or financial situation changes.

Exemption from withholding. If you are exempt, complete **only** lines 1, 2, 3, 4, and 7 and sign the form to validate it. Your exemption for 2009 expires February 16, 2010. See Pub. 505, Tax Withholding and Estimated Tax.

Note. You cannot claim exemption from withholding if (a) your income exceeds $950 and includes more than $300 of unearned income (for example, interest and dividends) and (b) another person can claim you as a dependent on their tax return.

Basic instructions. If you are not exempt, complete the **Personal Allowances Worksheet** below. The worksheets on page 2 further adjust your withholding allowances based on itemized deductions, certain credits, adjustments to income, or two-earner/multiple job situations.

Complete all worksheets that apply. However, you may claim fewer (or zero) allowances. For regular wages, withholding must be based on allowances you claimed and may not be a flat amount or percentage of wages.

Head of household. Generally, you may claim head of household filing status on your tax return only if you are unmarried and pay more than 50% of the costs of keeping up a home for yourself and your dependent(s) or other qualifying individuals. See Pub. 501, Exemptions, Standard Deduction, and Filing Information, for information.

Tax credits. You can take projected tax credits into account in figuring your allowable number of withholding allowances. Credits for child or dependent care expenses and the child tax credit may be claimed using the **Personal Allowances Worksheet** below. See Pub. 919, How Do I Adjust My Tax Withholding, for information on converting your other credits into withholding allowances.

Nonwage income. If you have a large amount of nonwage income, such as interest or dividends, consider making estimated tax payments using Form 1040-ES, Estimated Tax for Individuals. Otherwise, you may owe additional tax. If you have pension or annuity income, see Pub. 919 to find out if you should adjust your withholding on Form W-4 or W-4P.

Two earners or multiple jobs. If you have a working spouse or more than one job, figure the total number of allowances you are entitled to claim on all jobs using worksheets from only one Form W-4. Your withholding usually will be most accurate when all allowances are claimed on the Form W-4 for the highest paying job and zero allowances are claimed on the others. See Pub. 919 for details.

Nonresident alien. If you are a nonresident alien, see the Instructions for Form 8233 before completing this Form W-4.

Check your withholding. After your Form W-4 takes effect, use Pub. 919 to see how the amount you are having withheld compares to your projected total tax for 2009. See Pub. 919, especially if your earnings exceed $130,000 (Single) or $180,000 (Married).

Personal Allowances Worksheet (Keep for your records.)

A Enter "1" for **yourself** if no one else can claim you as a dependent . . . . **A** _____

B Enter "1" if:
- You are single and have only one job; or
- You are married, have only one job, and your spouse does not work; or
- Your wages from a second job or your spouse's wages (or the total of both) are $1,500 or less.

. . **B** _____

C Enter "1" for your **spouse**. But, you may choose to enter "-0-" if you are married and have either a working spouse or more than one job. (Entering "-0-" may help you avoid having too little tax withheld.) . . . . **C** _____

D Enter number of **dependents** (other than your spouse or yourself) you will claim on your tax return . . . . . . **D** _____

E Enter "1" if you will file as **head of household** on your tax return (see conditions under **Head of household** above) . **E** _____

F Enter "1" if you have at least $1,800 of **child or dependent care expenses** for which you plan to claim a credit . . **F** _____
(**Note.** Do **not** include child support payments. See Pub. 503, Child and Dependent Care Expenses, for details.)

G **Child Tax Credit** (including additional child tax credit). See Pub. 972, Child Tax Credit, for more information.
- If your total income will be less than $61,000 ($90,000 if married), enter "2" for each eligible child; then **less** "1" if you have three or more eligible children.
- If your total income will be between $61,000 and $84,000 ($90,000 and $119,000 if married), enter "1" for each eligible child plus "1" **additional** if you have six or more eligible children.

G _____

H Add lines A through G and enter total here. (**Note.** This may be different from the number of exemptions you claim on your tax return.) ► **H** _____

For accuracy, complete all worksheets that apply.
- If you plan to **itemize or claim adjustments to income** and want to reduce your withholding, see the **Deductions and Adjustments Worksheet** on page 2.
- If you have **more than one job** or are **married and you and your spouse both work** and the combined earnings from all jobs exceed $40,000 ($25,000 if married), see the **Two-Earners/Multiple Jobs Worksheet** on page 2 to avoid having too little tax withheld.
- If **neither** of the above situations applies, **stop here** and enter the number from line H on line 5 of Form W-4 below.

✄ - **Cut here and give Form W-4 to your employer. Keep the top part for your records.** -

Form **W-4**
Department of the Treasury
Internal Revenue Service

Employee's Withholding Allowance Certificate

► Whether you are entitled to claim a certain number of allowances or exemption from withholding is subject to review by the IRS. Your employer may be required to send a copy of this form to the IRS.

OMB No. 1545-0074

2009

1 Type or print your first name and middle initial.	Last name		2 Your social security number

Home address (number and street or rural route)

3 ☐ Single ☐ Married ☐ Married, but withhold at higher Single rate.
Note. If married, but legally separated, or spouse is a nonresident alien, check the "Single" box.

City or town, state, and ZIP code

4 If your last name differs from that shown on your social security card, check here. You must call 1-800-772-1213 for a replacement card. ► ☐

5 Total number of allowances you are claiming (from line **H** above **or** from the applicable worksheet on page 2) — **5** _____

6 Additional amount, if any, you want withheld from each paycheck . . . . — **6** $ _____

7 I claim exemption from withholding for 2009, and I certify that I meet **both** of the following conditions for exemption.
- Last year I had a right to a refund of **all** federal income tax withheld because I had **no** tax liability **and**
- This year I expect a refund of **all** federal income tax withheld because I expect to have **no** tax liability.

If you meet both conditions, write "Exempt" here . . . . ► **7** _____

Under penalties of perjury, I declare that I have examined this certificate and to the best of my knowledge and belief, it is true, correct, and complete.

Employee's signature
(Form is not valid unless you sign it.) ► _____

Date ► _____

8 Employer's name and address (Employer: Complete lines 8 and 10 only if sending to the IRS.)	9 Office code (optional)	10 Employer identification number (EIN)

For Privacy Act and Paperwork Reduction Act Notice, see page 2.   Cat. No. 10220Q   Form **W-4** (2009)

Notes

Notes

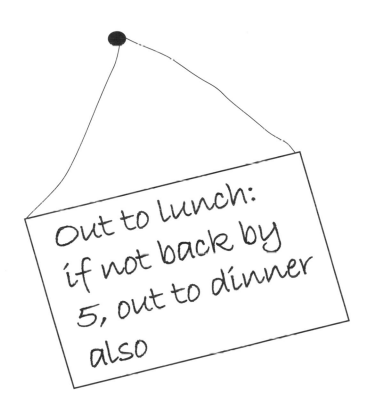

Hey, Get a Job!

There are a common list of skills and requirements for employees. This section discusses the things that make great employees, and those that are sure ways to get fired. These are true not only for teens, but for all workers young and old in any field. After reading through this section, the things your teachers are teaching you in school might make more sense.

> *An error of opinion may be tolerated where reason is left free to combat it.*
>
> *~Thomas Jefferson*

Technical Skills

- **Math** – Algebra seems to be an important math subject to employers because of the type of thinking you have to do in order to succeed at it.

- **Science** – Science not only provides the nuts and bolts behind everything, but it also requires study of problem solving and critical thinking.

- **Technology** – There are few jobs available today where you do not need to know how to use a computer.

- **Problem solving** – Not a problem solver, decision maker? You have a problem!

- **Critical thinking, logic** – Leave the drama, jumping to conclusions, faulty thinking at the door. Employers want rational people.

Communication Skills

- **Reading and Writing** - language arts classes, anyone?

- **Interpersonal skills** – no matter what job you do, there will always be a necessity to communicate and get along with other people.

Personal Traits/Attitudes

- **Hard working** – This would seem to be obvious, but people are fired for not working all the time.

> *Anne was a lazy student in school. When she passed a class, it was barely. Anne promised herself when she got a job her lazy ways would change. Anne was lucky enough to interview with an employer that didn't ask about her GPA. She got and started the job, but she and her employer discovered habits are extremely hard to break. She was fired because she didn't have a good work ethic.*

- **Dependable** – most often this is tied to lateness and absences without good reason. Attendance issues share the top spot for things people are fired for in this country. Businesses are strict, much stricter than your school when it comes to attendance. In order for an employer to benefit from your work, you have to be there.

> *Scott couldn't seem to make it to work on time. He was never more than 3 minutes late, but the company he worked for had a very strict policy. A note went into his file after he was late 2 times which meant he received no holiday bonus. After his 4th, he was fired.*

If you don't already use an agenda, you need to start. Don't depend on memory to keep track of school, work schedules and all your other activities. It will get to be too much. As a part time worker, your schedule could be different from week to week. To avoid costly mistakes, write things down.

Dependability also includes doing what you said you would, when you said you would do it. As you mature, more and more people will depend on you. If you want to have value, you can't check out physically or mentally and leave people hangin'.

Hard work spotlights the character of people: some turn up their sleeves, some turn up their noses, and some don't turn up at all.
~Robert Morely

- **Responsible** – Self motivated people are mature people. They are also the people who can make decisions and stand behind those decisions, good or bad. It's like Life Rule #6 – If you screw up, it's not your parents' (or anybody else's) fault so don't whine about your mistakes. Learn from them.

Barbara's employer knew his young employees would make mistakes. What he didn't expect was his inability to discuss those mistakes with Barbara. Each time he tried to teach her something about her job she interrupted him to explain why her mistake was someone else's fault. This grated on the nerves of her employer and her fellow employees until the employer was forced to let Barbara go.

In school, being responsible is really a suggestion. There's truthfully not a lot educators can do if you decide to do nothing. In the world of work, responsible employees are demanded. If you cannot meet that demand, you will not have a job.

- **Honesty and Integrity** – If these are not two of your qualities, then please don't get a job because you give all teenagers a bad name.

- **Flexibility and willingness** – Adapting to new situations and things you are asked to do is important. You are going into an entry level position which means you will do some things you don't like to do. We've all been there. Ask your parents about their first jobs. Have the ability to be willing and flexible in your job. Do the things you don't want to, pay your dues, and someday you won't be at the bottom. As Life Rule #5 says, Flipping burgers is not beneath your dignity. Your grandparents had a different word for burger flipping; they called it opportunity.

Jared was hired as a receptionist in a dentist's office. He wasn't told when he was hired that one of his responsibilities was to clean the bathroom. Jared refused when his boss told him to grab a toilet brush and get busy. He stated, "That's not what I was hired to do." Jared quit that job, but found that no matter where he went to work, he was expected to do tasks he didn't necessarily care for.

- **Respectful** - Without respect for others, you can't get along in the workplace. The inability to demonstrate respect shares the top spot with dependability for the reason people are fired. All jobs require you to be a member of a team. It can only be a team if there is respect between its members. And as you've probably been told a number of times, you can't get respect until you give it.

Chris knew copy machines very well. When his employer gave Chris and his fellow employees a big project to do, he emphasized the need to work as a team in order to meet the deadline. Chris didn't have respect for the others' ability to get things done. Chris tried to take over the project himself, ignoring another employee when she pointed out a typo to Chris. He was fired when he printed ten thousand business cards with a mistake on them.

- **Listening skills** - The ability to listen is closely related to many of the things I've already discussed, particularly respect. If you respect someone you will listen to them. Having good listening skills is essential to the workplace. People who are good listeners do the following:

   o Stop Talking – don't interrupt and don't finish other peoples' thoughts. These habits are annoying. Good listeners keep their mouths shut and their ears open.

   o Find something interesting about the other person. I hate to be the bearer of bad news, but not everything in this world is going to be entertaining. If you decide some thing is boring you won't listen. You could be missing something important. Good listeners find a way to tune in. Taking notes is one way to do that.

Listening Practice

   o Watch body language. Most of our communication comes through body language. If you want to get the message, you have to pay attention to it – listen between the lines, so to speak. If your boss says, 'I don't know what to with you,' with a smile, you know know it's much better than if he said it through gritted teeth.

   o Pay attention to your body language. Know that people are keying on you as well. If you have your arms folded tightly, or are slouching, or have no eye contact for example, you are demonstrating that you are not listening.

As a teacher there is nothing more frustrating than a student's refusal to listen. Irritation is really our only option. We can talk to the student or call their parent, but we can't just get rid of a student who doesn't listen. Employers, however, can fire the non-listener and find someone who will listen.

- **Positive attitude** - You can't be depressed, mad or moody while you are at work. Many of you will be working with customers who expect a positive attitude. Not to mention your fellow employees have to be around you too. A negative attitude in the workplace is like cancer in the body: it spreads. In order to return to health, the cancer has to be eliminated, just as the employee has to be fired.

Kara was having a lot of problems at home. Instead of embracing the time at work as a time to be away and think about something else, she stewed about the issues. Kara snapped at customers and her coworkers, and generally made everyone around her tired of her attitude. When her mood became so destructive that customers began to complain about her rude behavior, her employer fired her.

What it really comes down to is remaining an optimist rather than a pessimist. This is not an easy thing to do, particularly if there are negative things going on in your life. There are several choices you get to make on a daily basis; your attitude is one of them. For the sake of remaining employed, choose to have a positive attitude.

- **Life long learner** – If you've ever read your school's mission statement it probably includes something about creating life long learners. What this means is that you are willing and able to learn new things throughout your life. In other words, just because you get a diploma doesn't mean you're done learning. Jobs are going to require you to keep training, to keep learning. Otherwise you cannot advance within your company, or in some cases, even keep your job. My job as a teacher, at least as I see it, is not to cram information into a kid's head as much as it is to teach them to learn without me.

> *Thinking is the hardest work there is, which is probably why so few people engage in it.*
>
> *~Henry Ford*

- **Focus** – Employers need you to focus and pay attention to detail. Not only is this a need for quality in your work, but it's for your safety as well. Work accidents happen when employees lose focus.

> *Lee was not known for his ability to listen. He tended to daydream instead. He was doing just that when his boss was explaining the company's filing system to him. When she finished, she left Lee to file a stack of documents. He completed the task, but did it wrong. Needless to say, Lee's inability to focus lost him a job.*

 List the characteristics you need to work on.
Set goals to improve.

Much of success has to do with habits. What are you used to doing? Are you used to listening when being spoken to, is that your habit? Are you in the habit of completing tasks, or do you quit when you lose interest? If you want to experience success in life in general, you must form good habits. First jobs are not only building work history, but character as well. The decisions you are making today determine what kind of person you'll be. Does that mean there's no room for mistakes? Absolutely not.

I made bad decisions.

> *Work is either fun or drudgery. It depends on your attitude. I like fun.*
> *~Colleen C. Barrett*

I like the analogy of a person's life is like going for a walk. In the beginning, it is a smooth and level path. As we continue this walk through life, we begin to make our own decisions. The good decisions result in our path remaining smooth, or even becoming a downhill slope. Smart choices make our journey through life an easy one. Bad decisions, however, make our paths difficult. They make our walk an uphill challenge. Each negative choice makes the journey steeper. I have known many people, teens and adults, whose decisions made them into rock climbers. But the great thing about decision making is that we can always fix it. If we start making positive choices, our journey will become smooth again.

Keys for Keeping a Job

- Technical skills

- Communication skills

- Hard work, dependability, responsibility, honesty and integrity, flexibility and willingness, respect, listening skills, positive attitude, ability to learn, ability to focus

The Key to Success

If a man's called to be a street-sweeper he should sweep streets even as Michelangelo painted, or Beethoven composed music, or Shakespeare wrote poetry. He should sweep streets so well that all the host of heaven and earth will pause to say, 'Here lived a great street-sweeper that did his job well.'
~Martin Luther King

FAQs - What Do You Want From Me?

Do companies always have the 'customer is always right' point of view?

Only if they want to stay in business. You need to make your customers happy because that will make your boss happy.

Why are workplace romances not a good idea?

When we're in love, we tend to be very focused on our romance. Employers want you to focus on work, not your love interest. Besides that, romance tends to make your co-workers nauseous. Your flirting or PDA is harassment. There is also the possibility of a break up which makes you, your ex and everyone around you uncomfortable at work. Many companies have language in their handbooks specifically prohibiting interpersonal relationships at work.

Why do I need to give two weeks notice before quitting a job?

Because you want to be able to use that job as reference in the future. Therefore, you need to leave on good terms. That means that you give two weeks notice so the employer has time to replace you, and you do not leave them in a bad situation.

Is there a certain amount of time I have to work at a job?

If you want to use the experience on future job applications and résumés, yes. If the job was a summer job only, then the amount of time is going to be three months, and that's fine. But if it isn't a temporary job and you want to use the experience later, you probably need to stay at least six months. It doesn't look good on an application or résumé if you switch jobs a lot. Employers want to hire someone who is going to be around for a while.

Notes

Notes

Hey, Get a Job!

In order that people may be happy in their work, these three things are needed: *They must be fit for it. *They must not do too much of it. *And they must have a sense of success in it.

~John Ruskin

Most employers are admirable when working with teens. These are the bosses who aim to make working a positive, even fun experience for a teen. These are also the employers who schedule and pay their teen-aged employees fairly.

However, there is a minority who are not fair. These employers expect teens to be naïve enough to take whatever schedule and level of pay is offered to them, no matter how unjust.

William had a part-time job at a well-known department store. He liked the work and the people he worked with. William wanted to keep his grades up, but his employer scheduled him every week day for the closing shift. He didn't get home from work until late. The late hours made it difficult for William to keep up with school work, not to mention stay awake in class. William made a plea to his employer who seemed to get angry with him for wanting enough time to do better at school. However, the employer did stop scheduling William every night. Instead, he scheduled William every weekend and all holidays, including Christmas. When William asked for a day off, his boss threatened his job telling him he was too young and inexperienced to ask for days off. William persevered for a time thinking his employer would at least give him a raise for his hard work. According to company policies, he was due for a raise at six months.

William needed to realize his employer was taking advantage of him. A good boss will know you are a student, and in order to be successful in life, you need to do well in school. An employer you want will also remember teens need family time and time to have fun and be social.

A good employer rewards employees for their work. This could be a raise, a bonus, or maybe paid time off. If you're working hard, being dependable, all those attributes from the last section, you should feel a sense of success and pride. If instead you feel like a captive to your job, there is a problem.

How you can avoid bad employers:

- Ask questions about scheduling and requirements for promotion during your interview. Ask specifically about school nights, weekends and holidays.

- Ask somebody in the know. If you know anyone who works, or has worked for the business, ask them about work conditions and how the boss treated them. Places that have a high turn over rate (people quit often) may have it for a reason.

We're Always hiring!

- Know the labor laws for minors. Employers who will take advantage of teens are notorious for breaking these laws.

Most employers will work hard to keep their employees happy because they know happy employees work harder, and they stay.

> *Work is not man's punishment. It is his reward and his strength and his pleasure.*
>
> *~George Sand*

Don't take advantage of yourself. Confused? Read on, and it will become clear.

The point is, don't get wrapped up in the money. You're young and you need to have time for fun. There is plenty of time in your future to be tied down by work.

> *Sam was a senior in high school. She landed her first job at 15 doing clerical work.*
>
> *At 16, she bought a car. Her parents were not able to help her with the purchase, but they co-signed on a loan. Sam picked out a sporty little car at a price she thought she could handle. She admitted, however, that although she could cover the car payment, she completely forgot about the insurance, gas or maintenance for the car. Sam got a second part time job because she thought she needed the car as well as her top-of-the-line cell phone, ipod and name brand wardrobe.*
>
> *When Sam started her senior year, she was working two part time jobs and trying to graduate. There was a cost. Sam had a great car and great stuff, she even received a high school diploma, but she didn't have a life. Sam missed her senior year because she was working. She wanted to attend college, but realized she had no money saved up for college, and because of working, her grades weren't good enough for scholarships. Going to college would mean a third job and more loans.*

Graduation with my friends.

> *Never work just for money or power. They won't save your soul or help you sleep at night.*
>
> *~Marian Wright*

How to be Smart with Money:

- Open a savings account at the same time you open a checking account. Decide on a percentage of your check you're going to put into savings. I would suggest at least 25%. Even if you don't plan on going to college, I assume you want to move out of your parent's house at some point. That's expensive.

- Don't spend money you don't have. You are far too young to go into debt. If you want a car, save up the amount needed to buy that car. There are always unforeseen expenses later on, and you're in a much better position to handle those if you're not making a payment.

- Take time for you. Leave some time in your schedule for social activities with friends or family. Managing your time (like using an agenda) will actually help free up time for fun. Don't be that kid who realizes all they did in high school was work. It will be your biggest regret.

- Think in terms of experiences instead of things. How valuable something is has nothing to do with money, it has to do with experiences. Your first jobs are about experience. That's the important thing, not how many cool things you buy with the money you make. In our society, it is really hard to think this way, but when you are young it is so important for you to experience as much as you possibly can. You can't do that if your obsession is how much cool stuff you own. If this is you, there will come a time when you realize how empty that existence is and how much you've missed out on.

 Write down your short term and long term goals that will involve money. Set a budget in order to reach them.

Keys to a Fulfilling Job

- Know when an employer is taking advantage of you

- Deal with your money wisely

- Save some money

- Don't spend money you don't have

- Don't trade your experiences for material possessions

> *When it's time to die, let us not discover that we never lived.*
>
> *~Henry David Thoreau*

FAQs - In the Long Run

Do teenage employees get promotions and raises?
Absolutely. It takes time and money to train new employees, so employers want to keep you around. They know that if you are doing a good job you deserve to be rewarded with more responsibilities and more money. If you're doing an excellent job and you are not getting a promotion or a raise, you may want to ask yourself if an employer is taking advantage of you.

What are some things bosses will ask me to do when they're taking advantage of me?
Keep in mind that asking you to do things you don't like to do, cleaning toilet or pulling weeds for example, is not taking advantage of you. Having said that, anything that is dangerous for you to be doing, not getting deserved raises and promotions, or chronic disregard for child labor laws would indicate that you are being taken advantage of.

Can I get a job and buy a car without overdoing it?
Sure you can. Just don't expect to buy your dream car for your first car. Be patient and save the money you need for a car instead of getting yourself into a payment situation. If you need a car and you're going to have to make a payment, be smart with the length of the loan and the interest rate on the loan. And don't forget to factor in the cost of gas and maintenance. Some of you may have parents who will help you with a car. Parents are more willing to help if they see that you are going to pull your own weight financially.

Do I need to file a tax return?
Tax laws are ever changing, so I can't answer this question but the IRS can. Go to: www.irs.gov/individuals/students/index.html If you made enough money to file, you will file a 1040 EZ form.

What should I do if my employer is breaking the minor labor laws?
If they are putting you in danger, report them to the Department of Labor. Unfortunately, when it comes to working too many hours or working later than you are supposed to, the Department of Labor isn't going to do much. It's not worth your time to pursue. In these cases, it's up to you to decide whether you want to work there anymore.

THE END

Well, this is the end of the book. I hope it has been helpful. I am confident if you utilize this information you will be prepared to find, get and keep a job, all the while handling yourself in such a way you won't become a boring adult too soon.

Again, I would wish you luck, but in this case it won't do any good, so I will wish you good preparation.

Notes

Notes